A Fr

I want to say Thank You for buying my book so I put together a free gift for you!

"The Bean & Legume Desserts Cookbook"

www.GoodLivingPublishing.com/beans

This gift is the perfect complement to this book so if you want it sent to you just visit the link above.

Contents

Introduction

Beans and legumes are great, they really are…

Not only are they incredibly versatile and low cost, but they're also packed full of nutritious goodness - low in fat, high in protein, high in fibre and packed to the brim with folate, iron, potassium and magnesium means that beans and legumes truly are a superfood in a class of their own.

Their versatility means that they can easily be used for delicious breakfast, lunch and dinner recipes, and believe it or not, you can even whip up amazing desserts with them.

Simply adding a daily portion of beans or legumes to your diet is an excellent way to start losing weight, reducing your cholesterol, boosting your energy levels and generally becoming healthier. The nutritional make up of beans and legumes will leave you feeling fuller longer, increase your feeling of satiety and deliver a healthy dose of vitamins and minerals.

So, if you're on a diet, or just looking to be healthier, I would say that they are an essential food that you need to be eating.

In this book I've put together an awesome selection of recipes for you to make. Everything from breakfast dishes all the way to side dishes is covered, and every recipe is easy to cook and packed full of nutritious goodness. There are vegetarian dishes, meat dishes, soups, salads and (if you check out the free gift) even desserts.

A great thing about this book is that nearly every single recipe can have the beans or legumes switched out for the type you prefer more. Not a huge fan of pinto beans? No worries, just switch them for kidney beans, or black beans, or puy lentils… the recipe will still taste amazing.

If you've ever wanted to eat more beans and legumes then this book is essential for you. Over 45 simple yet delicious recipes that are all made with one of nature's most nutritious food types.

But that's not all, in the book I also cover the various beans and legumes available to you, the best way to prepare them and tips on cooking them perfectly.

So, turn the page and let's dive into the book.

I know you're going to love it…

Different Types of Beans & Legumes

Most supermarkets and grocery stores will stock a wide variety of beans and legumes, both in the dried form and canned. This chapter has a simple list of the most common beans and legumes that you will come across.

As I mentioned in the introduction, nearly all the recipes in the book can have the beans or legumes changed out for your personal taste preference.

So, experiment with the different options open to you and see what you like best.

Most Common Beans & Legumes

- Adzuki Beans

- Black Beans

- Black Eyed Peas

- Chickpeas

- Edamame

- Lentils

- Lima Beans

- Kidney Beans

Preparation & Cooking

Beans and legumes come as either canned goods or dried.

But, what is the difference between them?

Well, there is no nutritional difference between canned or dried, the main difference comes down to preparation. Canned beans and legumes are great when you're in a rush, just pop a can open, rinse in a fine-mesh sieve and drain.

Dried beans and legumes take a lot longer to cook, plus they need to be pre-soaked. I find that they are slightly tastier, but not by much.

So, really it comes down to your preference and how much time you have to spare.

If you choose to go the dried route, which many of the recipes in this book call for, you will need to soak your beans or legumes first.

The best way to do this is to add your dried beans or legumes to a pot and cover with water. Cover the pot and leave for 8+ hours, but ideally leave overnight. Drain them off in a sieve and rinse well.

When it comes to cooking a good idea is to cook up large batches in advance as they will keep for around 5 days in the refrigerator.

How to Cook

- Add the beans or legumes to a pot and cover with water.

- Place over a high heat and bring to the boil. Once boiling, reduce the heat to low, stir and cover.

- Let the pot simmer for anywhere between 30-45 minutes, stirring occasionally.

- Remove the cover 5 minutes before finished cooking time. *Optional: Season with sea salt and ground black pepper, stir to mix.*

If there is any water remaining in the pot then drain it off in a fine-mesh sieve. If more water is required during the cooking process add it ½ cup at a time. Follow the below section on "tips of cooking" for further information to make sure your dried beans and legumes cook perfectly every time.

Tips on Cooking

- Aim for around 3x the amount of water to beans and legumes.

- Add garlic, spices and herbs of your choice when cooking, add to the water and stir well.

- 1 lb. of dried beans/legumes will yield around 5-6 cups of cooked produce.

- You know they are properly cooked when you can easily mush one between your finger and thumb with only a little pressure.

- Don't add salt, or anything acidic, to the pot until almost finished cooking as it can dry the beans out if added too early.

Breakfast Recipes

Mexican Scrambled Eggs

Makes 2 Servings.

Ingredients

3 eggs, whisked

1 cup of pinto beans, cooked

½ cup of salsa

1" of chorizo, chopped into small pieces

1 clove of garlic, finely chopped

2 tbsp of lime juice

1 tbsp of olive oil

Directions

Place a pan over a medium heat and add the olive oil.

Once the oil is heated add the garlic and chorizo. Cook for 2 minutes, stirring frequently.

Add the whisked eggs, mix them with the garlic and chorizo. Cook for 1-2 minutes, until the eggs start to scramble. Be sure to keep them moving in the pan.

Add the pinto beans along with the salsa and fold into the eggs. Once well mixed you can let the eggs scramble to your liking.

Drizzle lime juice over before serving.

Chilaquiles

Makes1 Serving.

Ingredients

½ tbsp olive oil

3 small tortillas, cut into rough triangles

½ cup of hot salsa

¼ cup of pinto beans, cooked

1 large egg

¼ avocado flesh, cut into slices

2 tbsp grated cheddar

1-2 tbsp hot sauce

Directions

Place a pan over a medium heat and add the olive oil.

Once the oil is heated add the triangles of tortilla and cook for 4-5 minutes. Ensure you are continually turning them to prevent burning.

Add the beans, salsa and hot sauce, cook for 2 minutes, stirring frequently.

Push the contents of the pan to one side and crack the egg into the empty space.

Fry the egg and cook it as you like it.

Take off the heat. Spoon out the salsa tortilla mixture and lay it on a plate. Serve the avocado slices over this.

Carefully remove the egg and lay it over the avocado. Sprinkle the cheese over everything.

Lentil Vegetables

Makes 2 Servings.

Ingredients

1 cup of green lentils, uncooked

1 carrot, grated

1 zucchini, grated

3 tbsp of light soy sauce

Directions

Add the lentils to a pot and cover with 1-2" of water, place a medium-high heat underneath.

Bring to the boil then reduce the heat, cover and let simmer for 18-20 minutes.

Add the vegetables and stir into the lentils. Cover and cook for a further 2 minutes.

Drain any remaining water from the pot then add the soy sauce and gently stir together.

Breakfast Burrito

Makes 2 Servings.

Ingredients

½ cup of kidney beans, cooked

½ cup of chopped ham

3 eggs, whisked

2 tbsp of hot sauce

¼ cup of salsa

½ cup of grated cheddar cheese

2 whole-wheat tortillas

Ground black pepper, to taste

1 tbsp of butter

Directions

Place a pan over a medium heat and add the butter.

Once the butter is heated add the eggs and the hot sauce. Cook for 4-5 minutes, keep the eggs moving to scramble them.

As the eggs are cooking put the kidney beans, salsa and ham into a microwave proof dish. Heat in the microwave on high for 45 seconds.

Sprinkle the cheese into the kidney bean mixture and let it melt.

Microwave the tortillas for 5-10 seconds to soften. Spoon ½ of the egg mixture into each tortilla and then top with the kidney bean mix.

Season with pepper and then wrap up the tortillas.

Eggs & Beans

Makes 2 Servings.

3 eggs

1 egg yolk

1 cup of blacks beans, cooked

1 cup of spinach

Black pepper, to taste

2 pinches of sea salt

½ cup of salsa

Directions

Bring the 3 whole eggs to the boil in a pot of water. Let them hard boil, 4-5 minutes at a rolling boil, then peel and set aside.

In the now empty pot, add the black beans, spinach and black pepper. Heat over a medium-high heat until the spinach is wilted and everything is well mixed.

Add the egg yolk and stir into the mixture. Turn the heat to low and cook for 1 minute, stirring frequently.

As the egg yolk cooks in the black beans chop the hard boiled eggs into small pieces. Season the egg with the salt.

Add the egg pieces and salsa to the pot and mix everything together.

Apple Spiced Lentils

Makes 4 Servings.

Ingredients

1 cup of red lentils, uncooked

3 cups of red tea, brewed

2 apples, cored and diced

1 tbsp ground cinnamon

1 tsp ground turmeric

Maple syrup, to taste

Vanilla coconut milk, as needed

Directions

Add the lentils to a pot with the red tea. Bring to the boil over a medium heat.

Reduce the heat to low and let simmer for 8-10 minutes.

Add the apple slices and spices, stir well and then cook for a further 35-40 minutes.

Serve in a bowl with the coconut milk and drizzled with maple syrup.

Lentil & Coconut Power Bars

Makes 16 Bars.

Ingredients

½ cup of coconut oil

1 cup of whole-wheat flour

1 cup of all-purpose flour

1 cup of rolled oats

1 & ¼ cup of brown sugar

½ tsp salt

½ tsp baking soda

½ tsp cinnamon

1 cup of dried cranberries

1 cup of pecans, chopped or crushed

1 tsp ground ginger

½ cup of flaked coconut

1 15 oz. can of pumpkin

2 cups of green lentils, cooked and cooled

2 tsp vanilla extract

1 cup of dark chocolate chips

Directions

Preheat your oven to 350F and grease a 9x13" baking pan.

Mix together the flours, sugar, oats, cinnamon and baking soda. Once well mixed add the cranberries, nuts, ginger and coconut flakes, fold together.

In another bowl add the coconut oil, pumpkin, lentils and vanilla. Gently mix everything to combine.

Add the two mixtures together and stir to combine.

Once well mixed pour into the baking pan and press until even.

Bake until golden brown around the edges, around 30-35 minutes then remove and let cool.

Melt the chocolate chips and drizzle over the dish.

Cut into bars and store in the refrigerator.

Soups

Corn & Bean Chowder

Makes 4 Servings.

Ingredients

2 15 oz. cans of cream style corn

1 28 oz. can of kidney beans

1 onion, chopped

3 ribs of celery, thinly sliced

1 cup of vegetable broth

½ tsp thyme

1 bay leaf

½ tsp pepper

½ tsp of ground cayenne

Directions

Place a large pot over a medium heat.

Add all the ingredients to the pot and stir well.

Bring to the boil then cover, reduce the heat and let simmer for 30 minutes.

Remove the bay leaf before serving.

Tuscan Sundried Tomato Soup

Makes 4 Servings.

Ingredients

1 & ½ tbsp olive oil

1 onion, chopped

6 garlic cloves, sliced

2 tsp dried rosemary

1 bay leaf

½ tsp red pepper flakes

½ cup of sun-dried tomatoes, drained and chopped

1 carrot, chopped

2 16 oz. cans of garbanzo beans, drained

2 tbsp grated Pecorino cheese

Sea salt and pepper to taste

Directions

Place a pan pot over a medium heat and add the olive oil.

Add the garlic, onion, bay leaf, pepper flakes and rosemary to the pot and cook for 3 minutes, stirring frequently.

Add 2 cups of water, the tomatoes, 1 can of the beans, the carrot and bring everything to the boil.

Reduce the heat, cover and let simmer for 10 minutes. Remove the bay leaf.

Add the soup to a blender and pulse until smooth.

Return to the pan, add the remaining beans and cook for a further 5 minutes. Stirring occasionally.

Garnish with the grated cheese, salt and pepper.

Black Bean Soup

Makes 4 Servings.

Ingredients

2 15 oz. cans of black beans, undrained

1 16 oz. can of vegetable broth

½ cup of hot salsa

2 tbsp chili powder

1 tbsp grated Parmesan cheese

¼ cup of sour cream

Directions

Add 1 can of the beans to a blender and blitz until smooth.

Place a pot over a medium heat and add the smooth beans, the whole beans, the broth, the salsa and the chili powder. Bring everything to the boil, stirring occasionally.

Cover and let simmer for 5 minutes.

Stir in the sour cream and garnish with the cheese.

Ham & Lentil Soup

Makes 6 Servings.

Ingredients

1 medium-large ham hock

6 cups of water

1 & ½ cups of lentils

3 carrots sliced

1 cup of chopped celery

1 onion, chopped finely

1 tsp sugar

1 bay leaf

Sea salt and black pepper, to taste

Directions

Place a large pot over a medium heat then add the ham hock.

Add all the remaining ingredients and bring to the boil, stirring occasionally.

Reduce the heat, cover and let simmer for 55-65 minutes, the lentils should be tender.

Carefully take out the ham hock, remove any bone and shred the ham into small pieces.

Return the ham to the soup and stir well.

Season with more salt and pepper, to taste.

Slow Cooker Beef & Bean Soup

Makes 8-10 Servings.

Ingredients

1 lb. lean beef

2 14 oz. cans of chicken broth

1 can of diced tomatoes, undrained

7 green onions, sliced

3 carrots, sliced

2 ribs of celery, sliced

2 garlic cloves, minced

1 tbsp sugar

1 tsp dried basil

1 tsp sea salt

½ tsp oregano

½ tsp ground cumin

½ tsp chili powder

2 cans of black beans, drained

Directions

Place a pan over a medium heat and cook the ground beef for 8-10 minutes, stirring frequently. Make sure the beef is no longer pink.

Add the beef to a slow cooker then add all remaining ingredients, except the beans. Fold everything together to mix well then cover and cook on high for 60 minutes.

Turn the heat to low and cook for a further 4 hours.

Add the beans, stir in and cook on for a further 60 minutes.

Squash & Lentil Soup

Makes 6 Servings.

Ingredients

2 lbs. of butternut squash, seeds removed, peeled and chopped into chunks

1 & ½ cups of puy lentils

2 cups of vegetable stock

¾ cup of coconut milk

1 tbsp olive oil

1 onion, chopped

2 garlic cloves, minced

1 tsp ground ginger

1 tsp ground cumin

1 tsp ground coriander

1 tsp turmeric

1 tsp fennel seeds

Chopped cilantro, for serving

Sea salt, to taste

Directions

Place a large pot over a medium heat and add the olive oil.

Once the oil is heated add the garlic, onion and salt. Cook for 2-3 minutes stirring occasionally.

Add the remainder of the seasonings/spices and cook for a further 1-2 minutes.

Add the squash pieces, the stock, the lentils and fold everything together. Pour in enough water to cover everything.

Bring to the boil, cover and simmer for 35-40 minutes. You want the lentils and squash to be cooked through.

Take off the heat and stir in the coconut milk.

Sprinkle with chopped cilantro before serving.

Red Lentil Soup

Makes 2-3 Servings.

Ingredients

1 & ½ cups of red lentils

1 onion, chopped

1 tbsp olive oil

3 cups of vegetable stock

¼ tsp dried thyme

¼ tsp marjoram

Sea salt & ground black pepper, to taste

Directions

Place a pan over a medium heat and add the oil.

Cook the onion in the oil for 3-4 minutes, stirring occasionally.

Add the lentils then pour in the stock, stir and bring to the boil.

Reduce the heat and let simmer for 35 minutes.

If the soup is too thick add ½ cup of water and stir it in.

Add the thyme and marjoram, stir and cook for a further 2 minutes.

Season with salt and pepper.

Pumpkin Lentil Soup

Makes 2-3 Servings.

Ingredients

2 cups of red lentils

1 can of pumpkin puree

2 shallots, finely sliced

3 garlic cloves, sliced

1 leek, sliced

2 large tomatoes, chopped

½ tsp ground cinnamon

2 tsp of parsley

2 tbsp olive oil

Sea salt & ground black pepper, to taste

Directions

Place a large pan over a medium heat and add the olive oil.

Cook the garlic, shallots and leek in the oil for 2-3 minutes.

Add the lentils, pumpkin puree and cinnamon. Stir everything together until well mixed.

Pour in the water and add the tomatoes.

Bring to a boil, cover and reduce the heat to low. Cook for 25-30 minutes.

Add to a blender and pulse until smooth.

Return to the pot, heat through and then season with salt and pepper.

Pork & Kale Soup

Makes 4-6 Servings.

Ingredients

1 tbsp olive oil

1 lb. of pork tenderloin, cut into 1" pieces

1 onion, chopped

4 cloves of garlic, minced

2 tsp ground paprika, ideally use smoked paprika

½ tsp crushed red pepper flakes

1 cup of white wine

4 large tomatoes, chopped

4 cups of chicken broth

8 cups of kale, ribs removed, chopped

1 can of white beans, rinsed

Directions

Heat the olive oil over a medium-high heat in a large pan or soup pot.

Add the chopped pork and cook for 2-3 minutes, stirring frequently. Remove the pork from the pot and set aside, leave the juices in the pan. Turn the heat to medium.

Add the chopped onion and cook in the juices of the pork for 3-4 minutes. Mix in the garlic, smoked paprika and garlic, stir everything together and cook for 1 minute.

Pour in the wine and chopped tomatoes. Scrape the pan with your spoon to remove all browned bits, stir to mix everything together. Pour in the broth and increase the heat to high.

Bring to a boil then add the kale, reduce the heat and let simmer on a medium-low heat. Cook the kale for 5 minutes, stirring frequently, then add the pork and beans.

Stir well and cook for 2-3 minutes.

Salads

Black Bean Salad

Makes 6 Servings.

Ingredients

1 can of black beans, drained and rinsed

1 & ½ cups of frozen corn, defrosted

½ cup of chopped green onion

2 jalapeño peppers, seeded and chopped finely

3 large tomatoes, chopped

1 avocado, peeled, stone removed, and cut into chunks

¼ cup chopped basil

1 lime juiced

1 tbsp olive oil

1 tsp of sugar

Sea salt and ground black pepper, to taste

Directions

In a large bowl mix together all the ingredients except the sugar, pepper and salt.

Make sure salad is well tossed and mixed before sprinkling in the remaining ingredients.

Cannellini Bean Tuna Salad

Makes 4 Servings.

Ingredients

1 red onion, sliced

The juice and zest from 1 lemon and 1 lime

2 cans of tuna, drained

2 cans of cannellini beans, drained and rinsed

½ cup of chopped mint

4 splashes of Tabasco sauce

3 tbsp of olive oil

Sea salt and ground black pepper, to taste

Directions

Add all the ingredients to a large mixing bowl, except the olive oil, salt and pepper. Toss everything well.

Once the ingredients are well mixed season with the remaining ingredients and toss once or twice.

White Bean Cherry Tomato Salad

Makes 4 Servings.

Ingredients

1 can of white beans, drained and rinsed

2 cups of cherry tomatoes, halved

¼ cup of chopped parsley

1 tbsp of olive oil

Sea salt and ground black pepper, to taste

Directions

Add all the ingredients to a large mixing bowl and toss well.

Beetroot & Feta Salad

Makes 2 Servings.

Ingredients

2 tbsp olive oil

½ cup of beetroot

½ onion, chopped

1 red onion, chopped

1 cup of puy lentils, cooked

2 cups of spinach, torn

½ cup of feta cheese, crumbled or torn

Ground black pepper, to taste

Directions

Add the beetroot, onion, lentils and spinach to a large mixing bowl and toss well.

Add the feta cheese and gently toss to mix.

Season with the olive oil and black pepper.

Cranberry & Lentil Salad

Makes 4 Servings.

Ingredients

2 cups of green or puy lentils, cooked

½ cup of dried cranberries

½ cup of walnuts, chopped or crushed

½ cup of feta cheese, crumbled or torn

1 tbsp chopped parsley

3 tbsp olive oil

2 tsp lemon juice

2 tsp honey

Sea salt and ground black pepper, to taste

Directions

Add the lentils, cranberries, walnuts, lemon juice and olive oil to a large mixing bowl. Toss to mix well.

In a separate bowl gently mix together the honey and feta cheese.

Pour the cheese and honey over the salad and gently toss.

Season with salt and pepper.

Warm Chicken Balsamic Salad

Makes 4 Servings.

Ingredients

2 chicken breasts, cut into thin strips

2 garlic cloves, minced

2 tbsp wholegrain mustard

2 tbsp balsamic vinegar

1 tbsp of olive oil

1 can of cannellini beans, drained and rinsed

1 cup of cherry tomatoes, halved

1 red onion, chopped

1 red bell pepper, chopped

½ cup of feta cheese, crumbled

2 pressed cups of rocket leaves

Directions

Place a pan over a medium heat and add the olive oil.

Once the oil is heated add the garlic and chicken. Cook the chicken in the garlic, stirring frequently, for 3 minutes.

Add the balsamic vinegar, onion, pepper, tomatoes and beans. Mix everything to coat well and then cook for a further 4 minutes, or until the chicken is cooked through.

Take off the heat and add the mustard, toss well to ensure everything is well mixed.

In a large serving bowl add the cheese and rocket, toss well to mix.

Pour the contents of the pan, along with any juices, directly into the mixing bowl and toss well.

South-Western Chicken Bean Salad

Makes 4 Servings.

Ingredients

2 chicken breasts, cooked, cooled and cut into small pieces

1 can of black beans, rinsed and drained

1 cup of frozen corn, defrosted

2 scallions, chopped

½ red bell pepper, chopped

½ green bell pepper, chopped

2 tbsp lime juice

1 tbsp olive oil

2 tbsp taco or fajita seasoning

¼ cup sour cream

¼ cup of salsa

Directions

Add all the ingredients, except the sour cream, to a large mixing bowl. Toss everything together to mix well. A good tip is to add the taco seasoning one tsp at a time before tossing. This will ensure it is evenly distributed

Drizzle the sour cream evenly over the salad.

Avocado & Pinto Salad

Makes 3-4 Servings.

Ingredients

2 cups of pinto beans, cooked

2 large tomatoes, chopped

¼ cup chopped cilantro

2 scallions, thinly sliced

3 tbsp of lime juice

¼ cup of balsamic vinegar

1 avocado, stone removed, peeled, and chopped into chunks

Sea salt and ground black pepper, to taste

Directions

Add the pinto beans and balsamic vinegar to a large mixing bowl. Toss and then leave to sit for 60 minutes. Stir occasionally.

Add the remaining ingredients, gently toss everything together.

Main Meals

Body Warming Stew

Makes 5-6 Servings.

Ingredients

1 onion, chopped

1 tbsp olive oil

4 cloves of garlic, minced

1 28 oz. can of diced tomatoes, drained

3 carrots, chopped

3 ribs of celery, chopped

1 & ¼ cups of beef broth

1 tbsp Worcestershire sauce

1 can of kidney beans, rinsed and drained

1 can of chickpeas, rinsed and drained

1 can of black beans, rinsed and drained

1 small can of tomato paste

1 tbsp chili powder

Ground black pepper, to taste

Directions

Place a large pan over a medium heat and add the olive oil.

Cook the onions and garlic in the oil for 3 minutes. Add the tomatoes, celery, carrots, beef broth and Worcestershire sauce to the pan, bring everything to the boil.

Reduce the heat, cover and let simmer for 15-20 minutes.

Add the beans, tomato paste, pepper and chili. Stir everything together then cover and let simmer for a further 30 minutes, stir occasionally.

Chorizo Bean Stew

Makes 2 Servings.

Ingredients

8 oz. of chorizo, chopped

2 red onions, chopped

3 cloves of garlic, finely sliced

2 tbsp of olive oil

1 tsp of smoked paprika

1 can of tomatoes, diced

1 can of butter beans, rinsed and drained

Directions

Place a pan over a medium heat and add the olive oil.

Once the oil is heated add the chorizo, onion and garlic. Cook for 5 minutes, stirring occasionally.

Sprinkle the paprika in then add the tomatoes and beans. Reduce the heat to low, cover and let simmer for 20 minutes.

With 3 minutes to go remove the lid from the pan and let the stew thicken.

Black Pork Chops

Makes 4 Servings.

Ingredients

4 pork chops, ideally with the bone-in

1 tbsp olive oil

1 large can of black beans, undrained

1 cup of salsa

1 tbsp of chopped cilantro

Sea salt and black pepper, to taste

Directions

Place a large pan over a medium-high heat and add the olive oil.

Season the pork chops with pepper and salt.

Once the oil is heated add the pork chops and fry until brown on both sides.

Turn the heat to medium-low. Add the black beans and salsa, stir well to mix together.

Bring to the boil, reduce the heat then cover and let simmer for 25-30 minutes.

Season with the chopped cilantro.

Black Bean Quinoa

Makes 8-10 Servings.

Ingredients

1 tsp olive oil

1 onion, chopped

3 cloves of garlic, chopped

¾ cup of quinoa, uncooked

1 & ½ cups of vegetable broth

1 tsp ground cumin

½ tsp cayenne pepper

Sea salt and black pepper, to taste

1 cup of frozen corn kernels

2 cans of black beans, rinsed and drained

Directions

Place a pan over a medium heat and add the olive oil.

Cook the onion and garlic in the oil for 4 minutes.

Add the quinoa to the pan and mix well with the onion and garlic. Pour in the broth, then season with the spices and mix well.

Bring to the boil, reduce the heat to low then cover and let simmer for 20 minutes.

Stir in the corn and black beans to the pan, let cook for another 5 minutes.

Season with more salt and pepper to taste.

Lentil Stuffed Peppers

Makes 3 Servings.

Ingredients

6 green bell peppers

1 lb. of ground beef

1 onion, chopped

1 red bell pepper, chopped

6 cloves of garlic, minced

14 oz. of mild salsa

2 & ½ cups of cooked lentils

1 cup of grated cheddar cheese

Directions

Preheat your oven to 375F.

Cut the peppers in half lengthwise, scoop out any seeds and flesh inside. Lay them out on a baking dish and set aside.

Place a pan over a medium heat and add the olive oil.

Cook the garlic, red pepper and onion in the oil for 2 minutes then add the ground beef.

Ensure everything is well mixed and cook for 10 minutes, make sure the mince is browned all over.

Add the salsa, mix well and warm for 1 minute.

Take off the heat and add the lentils. Fold everything together to mix.

Spoon the lentil and beef mixture into the pepper halves. If you have any leftover just spoon into the baking dish around the peppers. Sprinkle cheese over everything.

Bake in oven for 20-25 minutes.

Lentil & Spinach Stew

Makes 4 Servings.

Ingredients

1 tbsp olive oil

3 onions, roughly chopped into large pieces

3 cloves of garlic, minced

½ cup of dried lentils

2 cups of water

10 oz. of frozen spinach

2 tsp ground cumin

Sea salt and ground black pepper, to taste

2 cloves of garlic, crushed

Directions

Place a pan over a medium heat and add the oil.

Cook the onion for 4 minutes then add the garlic. Stir well and cook for a further 5 minutes.

Add the lentils and water to the pan, mix well. Bring to the boil, reduce heat, then cover and let simmer for 30-35 minutes. You want the lentils to be tender, take off the heat at this point.

Defrost the spinach in the microwave and then add to the lentils. Fold everything together.

Season with the salt, pepper and cumin, mix well. Return to a low heat and cook for 5 minutes, stirring occasionally.

Add the crushed garlic over the top then season with salt and pepper before serving.

Pinto Bean & Ham Bake

Makes 4-6 Servings.

Ingredients

2 cups of pinto beans, dried

2 tbsp bacon drippings

1 onion, chopped

1 green bell pepper, chopped

12 oz. of chopped cooked ham

½ cup of ketchup

¼ cup of molasses

1 tbsp vinegar

2 tsp Worcestershire sauce

1 & ½ tsp dried mustard

½ cup of the reserved liquid beans cooked in

Sea salt, to taste

Directions

Cook the pinto beans in a pot of boiling water until tender, around 30-40 minutes. Drain the beans and set aside, be sure to reserve ½ cup of the water they were cooked in.

Preheat your oven to 325F.

Place a pan over a medium heat and add the bacon drippings. Cook for 30 seconds then add the onion and pepper, cook for 4-5 minutes, stirring frequently.

Take a casserole dish and create a base layer with the pinto beans. Add the onion and pepper mixture evenly over the top.

Create the next layer with the chopped ham. Sprinkle in the sea salt, to taste.

Mix together all the remaining ingredients in a bowl then pour evenly over the casserole dish.

Bake in the oven for 60 minutes.

Bean Quesadillas

Makes 4 Servings.

Ingredients

½ onion, finely chopped

2 cloves of garlic, minced

1 can of black beans, rinsed and drained

1 courgette, chopped

1 tsp ground cayenne

1 tsp red chili flakes

½ green bell pepper, chopped

2 large tomatoes, chopped

4 (12") flour tortillas

⅓ cup of shredded cheddar cheese

2 tbsp olive oil

Directions

Place a pan over a medium heat and add 1 tbsp of olive oil.

Cook the garlic and onion in the oil for 4-5 minutes.

Add the pepper, beans, chopped tomatoes, courgette and chili flakes. Cook for 4-6 minutes, stirring frequently.

Place a new pan over a medium heat and add ½ tbsp of the olive oil. Add 1 tortilla to the pan and then spoon half of the bean mixture onto it. Sprinkle with ½ of the cheese and then lay another tortilla over it.

Cook for 1-2 minutes then carefully flip the quesadilla and repeat.

Repeat with the remaining tortilla and bean mixture.

Cut the quesadillas into wedges before serving.

3 Bean Chilli Classic

Makes 6 Servings.

Ingredients

2 lbs. of lean ground beef

2 tbsp olive oil

1 onion, chopped

1 green bell pepper, chopped

1 red bell pepper, chopped

2 cloves of garlic, minced

1/3 cup of chili powder

2 tbsp ground cumin

1 can of pinto, kidney and black beans

1 10 oz. can of tomato sauce

1 can of diced tomatoes

Ground cayenne to taste

Sea salt and ground black pepper, to taste

Directions

Place a large pot over a medium heat and add the olive oil.

Cook the garlic and onion for 4 minutes, stirring frequently, then add the ground beef.

Mix everything together and cook for 8-10 minutes ensuring the beef is browned all over. Keep stirring frequently.

Add the peppers, chili powder and cumin. Mix until the meat is well coated.

Add the tomato sauce, diced tomatoes, 1 & ½ cups of water and the 3 cans of beans to the pot. Mix everything well and continue stirring for 1-2 minutes.

Sprinkle in the cayenne, salt and pepper then reduce the heat, cover and let simmer for 30 minutes. Stir occasionally.

Lentil Quiche

Makes 6-8 Servings.

Ingredients

½ cup of dried lentils

1 onion, chopped

2 tbsp olive oil

2 cups of water

2 cups of broccoli florets

2 large tomatoes, chopped

4 eggs, beaten

1 cup of milk

Sea salt and ground black pepper, to taste

2 tsp Italian seasoning

½ cup of cheddar cheese, grated

Directions

Preheat your oven to 375F.

Place a pan over a medium heat and add the olive oil.

Cook the onion in the oil for 5 minutes then add the lentils and water. Stir everything together and bring to the boil.

Reduce the heat to low, cover and let simmer for 18-20 minutes.

Add the broccoli to the lentils, fold to combine and then cook for a further 5 minutes. If any water remains drain it off. Cook the lentils for 1-2 minutes in the pan to ensure they are dried off.

Pour the mixture into a casserole dish and top with the cheese.

Mix together the eggs, Italian seasoning, salt, pepper and milk then pour into the casserole dish.

Bake for 40-50 minutes. Let cool for 4 minutes before serving.

Flaked Lemon Lentils Fish

Makes 2 Servings.

Ingredients

1 cup of dried lentils

1 onion, finely chopped

1 carrot, finely chopped

1 celery stick, finely chopped

2 cups of vegetable stock

1 tbsp half-fat crème fraiche

1 tbsp chopped dill

The zest of ½ a lemon

2 white fish fillet

1 cup of baby spinach

Directions

Add the lentils to an oiled pan with the chopped onion, carrot and celery and place over a medium heat.

Add the stock and bring to the boil. Stir a few times and reduce the heat. Cover and let simmer for 30 minutes

In a bowl mix the crème fraiche, ½ of the dill and the zest.

Lay the fish in a shallow microwave proof dish with 3 tbsp of water and cover with cling film leaving one corner open slightly.

Microwave on medium for 4-6 minutes until the fish flakes easily when touched with a fork. Flake the fish with a fork.

Once the lentils are tender, add the spinach and stir. Continue to cook at a low heat and add the crème fraiche once the spinach has wilted.

Serve and top with flaked fish. Garnish with the remaining dill.

Cod & Chorizo Stew

Makes 4 Servings.

Ingredients

4 pieces of cod, skinless

1 tbsp olive oil

1 onion, chopped

2" of chorizo, chopped

2 cloves of garlic, minced

½ can of diced tomatoes

1 can of tomato sauce

1 can of cannellini beans, drained

1 & ½ cups of shredded green cabbage

½ tsp sugar

Sea salt and ground pepper, to taste

Directions

Place a pan over a medium heat and add the olive oil.

Cook the onion in the oil for 4 minutes then add the chorizo and garlic. Cook for 2-3 minutes, stirring frequently.

Add the tomatoes, tomato sauce, cabbage and sugar. Stir well and let cook for 2 minutes.

Place the cod in the pan and surround/cover the fillets with the sauce. Turn the heat to medium-low, cover and cook for 5 minutes.

The fish should flake easily with a fork.

Season with salt and pepper, to taste.

Crusted Salmon

Makes 4-6 Servings.

Ingredients

5 tsp olive oil, divided

1 bulb of fennel, halved, core removed, thinly sliced

1 tbsp chopped fennel fronds

2 cans of white beans, rinsed

2 large tomatoes, chopped

1/3 cup of dry white wine

1 tbsp Dijon mustard

1 tbsp fennel seeds

4-6 salmon fillets, skinless

Ground black pepper, to taste

Directions

Place a pan over a medium heat and add 2 tsp of the olive oil. Throw in the sliced fennel and cook for 5-6 minutes, stirring frequently.

Add the beans, chopped tomatoes and white wine. Cook for 3-4 minutes, stirring frequently. The tomatoes should be broken down.

Transfer the contents of the pan to a bowl and mix with fennel fronds, pepper and mustard seeds. Cover and set aside.

Add the remaining oil to the pan and warm over a high heat.

Once the oil is warm add the salmon fillets to the pan and cook for 3-4 minutes before flipping, turning the heat to low and covering. Cook for 2-3 minutes, covered, on low.

Serve the salmon on top of the white bean mixture (if it needs heated just quickly add to a pot and heat for 1 minute).

Bean Chipotle Chilli with Crispy Fritters

Makes 2-3 Servings.

Ingredients

1 tbsp olive oil

1 onion, finely chopped

2 cloves of garlic, minced

1 tsp ground cumin

1 tsp chipotle chili powder

1 tsp thyme

1 tsp cayenne pepper powder

1 tomato, diced

1 can of black beans, drained and rinsed

2 cups of vegetable stock

1 tbsp fresh lime juice

For the Fritters:

1 zucchini, grated

½ tsp salt

1 egg

½ cup of bread crumbs

1 tbsp pine nuts

1 tsp lime zest

1 tsp lime juice

1 tbsp oil

Directions

Add the oil to a large pot and place over a medium heat.

Cook the onion and garlic in the oil, stirring frequently, for 4-5 minutes. Mix in the cumin, thyme, cayenne powder and chilli powder. Stir everything to mix well.

Add the tomato and cook for 5 minutes, stirring frequently. Pour in the black beans along with the stock and bring to the boil, stirring frequently. Reduce the heat to low and let simmer.

As this cooks begin to make the fritters by adding the zucchini, pine nuts, zest, breadcrumbs and egg to a bowl. Mix well to combine everything.

Place another pan over a medium heat and add the olive oil.

To make a fritter add a dollop of the zucchini mixture to the pan, flatten with your spatula and fry for 5 minutes before flipping and cooking for another 5 minutes. Repeat until all the mixture has been used.

Add the lime juice to the black bean mixture then serve the fritters on top of the beans.

Collard Greens Chicken

Makes 6 Servings.

Ingredients

1 & ½ cups of dried lima beans

1 tbsp olive oil

2 red onions, chopped

3 cups of chicken broth

6 oz. of chicken breast, chopped

½ tsp dried thyme

¼ tsp crushed red pepper

3 cloves of garlic, minced

1 bay leaf

8 cups of chopped collard greens

2 tbsp red wine vinegar

1 can of diced tomatoes, undrained

Sea salt and ground black pepper, to taste

Directions

Add the beans to a dutch oven along with enough water to cover 2" above them. Bring to the boil over a medium-high heat.

Reduce the heat to medium-low, cover and cook for 20-25 minutes. Take off the heat and drain.

Preheat your oven to 375F.

Add the olive oil to the pan and place over a medium heat.

Add the onion and cook for 4-5 minutes, stirring frequently.

Add the beans, the broth and the next 5 ingredients in the list. Bring this to a boil then cover and transfer the dutch oven/pan to the oven. Cook for 75-80 minutes.

Add the collard greens, red wine vinegar, can of tomatoes and stir everything together well. Return to the oven and cook for a further 60 minutes. Stir occasionally.

Season with salt and pepper, remove the bay leaf before servings.

Broccoli Bean Curry

Makes 4 Servings.

Ingredients

3 cups of dried kidney beans

4 tbsp butter

2 onions, chopped

1 tsp chili powder

2 tsp cumin

1 tsp ground coriander

2 tsp turmeric

1 lemon, juiced

3 cups of chicken broth

2 heads of broccolis, chopped

1 tbsp flour

1 cup of cashews, chopped or crushed

Black pepper, to taste

Directions

Add the butter to a pan and cook over a medium heat. Add the onion once the butter has melted and cook for 4-5 minutes.

Sprinkle in the chili powder, pepper, cumin, coriander and turmeric. Mix well and cook 1-2 minutes.

Add the kidney beans, lemon juice and broth. Stir everything to mix well and then bring to the boil. Reduce the heat and let simmer for 50 minutes. If it thickens too much add ½ cup of hot water.

Steam the broccoli in a covered pot with 2" of water in it. Steam for 8 minutes, or until a fork easily pierces the florets, then drain.

Remove ½ a cup of liquid from the bean mix. Add the flour to this and mix well to form a smooth paste. Pour the paste, broccoli and nuts into the curry mixture and stir well. Cook for a further 2 minutes.

Bean, Chocolate and Nut Chilli

Makes 4 Servings.

Ingredients

2 tbsp olive oil

1 onion, chopped

2 garlic cloves, finely chopped

2 tsp cumin seeds

1 fresh red chilli, minced

1 tsp ground paprika

1 tsp dried oregano

2 bell peppers, chopped

1 carrot, chopped

1 parsnip, finely chopped

2 large celery stalks, finely chopped

½ cup of walnuts, crushed or chopped

28 oz. of cooked mixed beans

2 16oz. cans of whole plum tomatoes

1 cup of water

½ cup of red wine

2 oz. of dark chocolate, crumbled

Sea salt and black pepper, to taste

For serving

½ cup of plain yoghurt

Coriander, coarsely chopped

1 lime, quartered

4 tortillas, lightly toasted

Directions

Add the oil to a large pot and place over a medium heat.

Add the onion, garlic, cumin, paprika, chilli and oregano. Cook for 4 minutes stirring frequently.

Mix in the peppers, carrot, parsnip and celery. Cook for 3 minutes, ensure everything is well mixed and vegetables are coated.

Add the water, tomatoes, beans and the nuts. Cook for 25-30 minutes stirring frequently.

Pour in the red wine and chocolate, stir everything together and cook for 5 minutes. Season with salt and pepper.

When it comes to serving dollop the yoghurt over the chilli, sprinkle with coriander and give a lime wedge with each portion.

Lasagne

Makes 8 Servings.

Ingredients

1 tbsp olive oil

2 onions, chopped

4 cloves of garlic, chopped

½ green bell pepper, chopped

½ red bell pepper, chopped

1 15 oz. can of chopped tomatoes

1 cup of hot salsa

2 cans of black beans, rinsed and drained

2 avocados peeled and mashed up

1 tbsp lemon juice

12 6" tortillas, quartered

2 cups of cheddar cheese, grated

Directions

Preheat your oven to 400F. Grease a 9x13" baking dish and set aside.

Place a pan over a medium heat and add the olive oil.

Once the oil is heated add the onions, garlic and pepper, cook for 4-5 minutes, stirring frequently.

Add the tomatoes, salsa and the beans. Mix everything together and bring to the boil, reduce the heat and let simmer for 4 minutes.

Mash together the avocado and lemon juice.

Create a base layer in the baking dish with some of the tortilla pieces. Spread 1/3 of the bean mixture onto this. Spoon in some of the avocado and sprinkle with the cheese. Repeat this layer-by-layer until all the ingredients have been used.

Bake in over for 35-40 minutes.

Sides

Slow Cooked Tomato Beans

Makes 6 Side Servings.

Ingredients

For the beans

1 cup of white beans, dried

6 cups of water

1 carrot, chopped

1 onion, chopped

½ tsp ground thyme

½ tsp ground rosemary

1 tbsp sea salt

For the tomato sauce

3 slices of bacon, chopped into small pieces

¼ cup of olive oil

1 onion, chopped

4 cloves of garlic, finely chopped

½ tsp sea salt

1 lb. of tomatoes, chopped

½ cup of canned tomato purée

Directions

Add the beans, along with all the ingredients in that section (except the salt) to a pot and bring to the boil. Reduce the heat to low, cover and let simmer for 40 minutes. 5 minutes before the finishing time add the salt and stir well.

As the beans cook make the tomato sauce.

Place a pan over a medium heat and fry the chopped bacon until crispy.

Pour in the olive oil, onion and garlic. Cook for 4 minutes, stirring frequently.

Add the tomatoes, the puree and the salt. Stir everything together and then bring to the boil.

Reduce the heat, cover and let simmer until the sauce begins to thicken, 20-25 minutes.

Drain the beans and combine all the ingredients together. Make sure everything is well mixed.

Dirty Spice Rice

Makes 6 Side Servings.

Ingredients

2 tbsp olive oil

3 garlic cloves, minced

1 chopped onion

1 green bell pepper, chopped

1 tbsp chili powder

2 tsp annatto powder

¼ tsp crushed red pepper flakes

1 tsp ground cumin

¼ tsp ground cinnamon

1 & ½ cups uncooked white rice

3 cups of water

3 large tomatoes, chopped

1 can of black beans, rinsed and drained

¼ cup of toasted pine nuts

1 red onion, sliced

1 tbsp lime juice

Directions

Place a large pan over a medium heat and add 1 tbsp of the olive oil.

Add the garlic and onion. Cook for 4-5 minutes, stirring frequently.

Add the pepper, chili powder, chili flakes, annatto, cinnamon and cumin. Cook for 2-3 minutes stirring continually.

Mix in the rice and ensure it is well coated. Once everything is well mixed add the water and a sprinkling of sea salt.

Bring the boil then reduce the heat, cover and let simmer for 23-25 minutes.

Once the rice is cooked and the water is all gone add the tomatoes, red onion, cilantro, black beans, pine nuts and remaining olive oil. Mix everything together and cook for 3-5 minutes, or until everything is heated through.

Drizzle the lime juice over the top.

Sun Dried Tomato Bean Dip

Ingredients

1 can of white beans, rinsed and drained

1 onion, chopped

4 tbsp olive oil

1 clove of garlic, chopped

2 sage leaves, torn

6 sun-dried tomatoes, finely chopped

1 tbsp capers

1 tsp paprika

Juice from half a lemon

Sea salt and ground black pepper to taste

Directions

Add 1 tbsp of the olive oil to a pan and cook the onion and garlic over a medium heat.

Cook for 5 minutes, stirring frequently.

Add all remaining ingredients, except the sundried tomatoes, including the contents of the pan to a blender and pulse until smooth.

Return to the pan, add the tomatoes and cook, stirring frequently, for 5 minutes.

Serve warm or cold.

Curried Kidney Beans

Makes 6-8 Side Servings.

Ingredients

1 bunch of mustard greens

2 tbsp of butter

2 shallots, chopped

1 tsp ground ginger

1 tsp red pepper flakes

1 can of kidney beans, rinsed and drained

1 15 oz. can of tomato sauce

2 tsp curry powder

½ cup of half and half

Directions

Add the greens to a large pot of boiling water, cover and cook for 8-10 minutes. Drain and set aside.

Place a pan over a medium heat and melt the butter.

Add the shallots and fry for 4 minutes, stirring frequently. Sprinkle in the ginger and mix well.

Add the greens, kidney beans, tomato, pepper flakes and curry powder to the pan. Fold everything together well and cook for 2 minutes, stirring continually.

Pour in the half & half and mix well. Cook for 4 minutes stirring frequently.

Potato-less Potato Salad

Makes 8 Servings.

Ingredients

1 red bell pepper, finely chopped

2 scallions, finely sliced

1 rib of celery, chopped

1 tbsp chopped cilantro

1 cup of mayonnaise

2 chipotle chillies, deseeded and finely sliced

½ tsp sugar

6 slices of bacon, cooked crisp and crumbled

1 can of black beans, rinsed and drained

4 hard-boiled eggs, chopped

1 can of chickpeas, rinsed and drained

Sea salt and black pepper, to taste

Directions

Mix together all the ingredients in a large bowl. Make sure everything is well tossed.

Season with salt and pepper, to taste.

Garlic & Spice Lentils

Makes 4 Servings.

Ingredients

1 & ½ cups of dried lentils

2 tbsp ground garlic

2 tbsp ground smoked paprika

1 tbsp butter

Sea salt and ground black pepper, to taste

Directions

Add the lentils to a pot and cover with 2-3" of water.

Bring to the boil over a medium-high heat. Reduce the heat to low, cover and let simmer for 15 minutes. Stirring occasionally.

If more water is required add it ½ cup at a time.

Add the remaining ingredients and fold everything well. Continue to let simmer for 10 minutes, stirring occasionally.

Remove the cover and cook for 5 minutes. Season with salt and pepper and fold in.

Enjoy this book?

Please leave a review and let others know what you liked about this book.

Reviews are so crucial to the success of an authors and even one quick sentence review would mean the world to me!

Lots of Love

Sarah

Printed in the USA
CPSIA information can be obtained
at www.ICGtesting.com
LVHW010231080324
773912LV00021B/339